Help Find Baby Jesus

Follow the path and find the new king as
the Magi did in Matthew 2:1-9.

Bible Mazes

Help Find the Promised Land

Follow the path through the plagues God sent to Pharaoh to free his people as in Exodus 9–11.

Help Thank Jesus

Follow the path to help the Leper thank
Jesus as told in Luke 17:12–19.

Help Find Bethlehem

Follow the path to help Mary and Joseph find
a place to stay as in Luke 2:1–7.

Help Zaccheus

Follow the path to help Zacchaeus be
with Jesus as in Luke 19:1–9.

Help the Children Get to Jesus

Follow the path to help the children get to
Jesus as they did in Luke 18:16.

Help Jonah Out

Follow the path to help the big fish
spit Jonah onto dry land as in Jonah 2:1–10.

Bible Mazes

Help Bring Good News

Follow the path to help the angel proclaim the birth of
Jesus to the shepherds as in Luke 2:8-14.

Help Find the Ark

Follow the waves to get the news of dry land to
the ark as the dove did in Genesis 8:6–12.

God takes care of you!

Bible Mazes

Help Find the Lost Sheep

Follow the path to find the lost sheep as the Shepherd did in Matthew 18:10–14.

Help Wear the New Coat

Follow the path through the coat Joseph received
from his father as in Genesis 37:3.

Help the Raven Get to Elijah

Follow the path to help feed Elijah
as in 1 Kings 17:1-6.

Help the Snake Talk to Eve

Follow the snake to speak to Eve
as it did in Genesis 3:1–14.

Bible Mazes

Help the Son Get Home

Follow the path to help the son return
home as he did in Luke 15:11–32.

Help Solomon Receive Wisdom

Follow the path to the wisdom Solomon
prayed for in 1 Kings 3:9–12.

Help the Boy Put on Armor

Follow the path to help the boy collect and put on the
Armor of God as in Ephesians 6:13-18.

Help Rescue Moses

Follow the path to find baby Moses as the
Pharaoh's daughter did in Exodus 2:5–10.

Bible Mazes

Help Make David King

Follow the path to crown David king over the
house of Judah as in 2 Samuel 2:1–7.

Complete the Rainbow

Follow the path to remind us of the promise
God made in Genesis 9:13–16.

Help the Fish Reach the Net

Follow the waves to fill the net with fish
as Jesus did in Luke 5:1–7.

Help the Boy Get to His Basket

Follow the path to help feed 5,000 people
as Jesus did in John 6:9–11.

Help Crumble Walls

Follow the path around the city of Jericho as
Joshua and his people did in Joshua 6:1–5.

Help Find the Coin

Follow the path through the house to find the
lost coin as the woman did in Luke 15:8–10.

Help David Play His Harp

Follow the path to help David play his soothing music
to King Saul as he did in 1 Samuel 16:23.

Help Find Jesus

Follow the path to help Jesus' parents
find him as in Luke 2:41–52.

Talking to your friends about Jesus is fun!

Help the Women Get to Jesus

Follow the path to the Risen Lord as the
women did in Matthew 28:1–10.

Help Cross the Red Sea

Follow the path to dry land as the
people did in Exodus 14:13–22

Help Find Five Stones

Follow the path to help David get the stones for his slingshot as he did in 1 Samuel 17:1-47.

Help the People Worship Jesus

Follow the path to meet Jesus as
they did in John 12:12–18.

Help Calm the Storm

Follow the waves to calm the storm and the
worried disciples as in Matthew 8:23–27.

Help Two Sisters Get to Their Brother

Follow the path to the risen Lazarus
as in John 11:38–44.

Help Find the Inn

Follow the path to get help as the Good
Samaritan did in Luke 10:25–37.

Bible Mazes 02121